Lyrics From The Chamber

by
Mark McConville

Close To The Bone Publishing

Contents

About the Author

◆

Mark McConville is a freelance music journalist from a tiny town called Carluke in Lanarkshire Scotland. He began to write music reviews and features in 2013, for online and print publications. His love for poetry stems from the struggles he feels day to day, the impact of loss, and his battles with his own mental health.

Lyrics From The Chamber

Bleak Cocoon

There's a lack of light here
Inside this room which used to be vibrant
She's looking at those stars in a sky she wants to
pull down
So she can drape it over her skin.

Tonight we're standing on the edge
Preparing for riots to overwhelm our heads
Gunshots ring out on the streets
Enemies of the world cause mayhem
As we tend to our itchy wounds.

We exposed the killer in our nightmares
He's an ugly tyrant, forcing us to,
Feed on the scraps of our youth.

Outside this bleak cocoon
Is a world beyond this one?
A utopia with clean oxygen
And no smoky avenues.

Sick to the stomachs that,
Keep our organs in check
We think about death more than
Our sinking souls.

Drunken Bodies

The spotlight on me
Capturing my tired eyes
I'm in a room full of drunken bodies
They slur about the end of the world
And their hopes and dreams
Are filtered out by intoxication and excuses.

I stand in the doorway
Observing men managing to keep their heads
upright
Their livers screaming for the comforts of restraint
The house is a prison for a vital organ.

The roses are dead, submerged in dirty water,
They had body and color, they were a gift,
A token of love, for who we don't know?

The lifeless gain energy
Drinking whiskey and monitoring
The bloom of love
As youth kiss chapped lips
They're kissing to stay alive
As the alcohol takes control
A behemoth with red lit eyes.

The window begins to turn colorful
Blue covers the room, hearts frightened
Cops barge open doors in a rough embrace.

The light is blinding, the music,
The bellowing front-man through loud speakers
It all becomes quiet, subtle and calm,
The Party is over.

Colourless Eyes

I walk the line
Through rainstorms and bitter conflicts
Hastily drinking from a bottle concealed in a paper-
bag
Brushing with death in every alleyway I walk
through
Counting change and veins in my arms.
Colourless eyes staring, gazing into mine,
I'm in hell on earth, but I only know such chaos.
I'm one of them, startling people, fracturing my
chance of
A resurgence when hope skids on thin ice that
covers the ground
The enemy fearless in their pursuit of my last claim
to gold.
I have no reason to fight either, I have demons for
that, and they're justified
Killers, psychologically enforcing their imprint.

Cinematic Realization

In the beginning
Your innocence was drained from you
Taken away from your hourglass body
Profoundly stripped from your grasp
This light is flickering over here
And you're stuck in the darkness
I can see glitter and a hand.

You stretch forward and show the other hand
In it is a red apple, a glorified color,
But the crimson is striking
And you redefine beauty
Captivating me and the lonely ghost.

The phantoms are here
Swirling and screaming
Around us is tension
Masterminded conversations
Echoing in this coliseum of broken foundations.

I stand
Building up a resistance
Spotting young moths
Surrounding the fading lightbulb.

Youth isn't on our side
We're edging close to middle part
Of our lives.
The light becomes a beacon
We see our future on dusty movies
In this cinematic realization
You are the natural color to my grey face.

You come closer
I now see you in full bloom
Mastering the art of a seduction
Cries aren't as deafening here
These spirits are clapping their ghostly hands.

We have a direct route into majestic territories
Mascara tears are halted, your eyes,
Gleaming in an artist's dream
Through the eyes of this generation
We're lovers escaping the loud noises,
And insulting voices, we're the dreamers,
Waltzing on and disarming our own alarming
minds.

Breathing Loudly For God To Hear

Love has no intentions
Anxiety holds my hand
And there's church bells ringing outside,
A marriage has taken place
Beautiful parades follow
And I'm corrupted by sorrow ridden hopelessness.

She's a stylish bride, wearing white,
The connection between her and him is strong
A bond unbreakable, and there's me with saturated
eyes,
Watching on like an onlooker envious of what he's
witnessing,
Flowers thrown, kisses granted, hope building its
puzzle.

I turn away and look on at this room
Covered in cigarette burns and smashed glass
Dust and poetic ramblings on brown paper,
There's no one here but me, wishing that the ceiling
would open up,
To reveal an eloquent picture of two lovers clasping
hands and kissing
Life into the world.

I'm sad, there's no doubt,
Feeling dread come over me like a dark cloud
I forage for some pills for a damning headache
Breathing loudly for God to hear.

I would depart this room, disguise myself,
Loot the piggy bank and purchase Vicodin and a
bottle,
Of the cheapest wine, 15% of misery, but hell is
brewing,
And I'm desperate for relief.

But I'm too much of a fool
A spectator never edging closer to wonderment.

So I'll sit fearing that the walls will melt
And conceal me and these half-hearted writings.

Fountain Of My Poison

Forget me my darling
As I try to resolve the situation
My hands are shaking
My mind is needy
I hope to live for one more minute or so
To see you leave with a smile upon your face.

The bottle stared me down
I smashed it upon a stone
It almost cut through my arms
To feel the pain and the blood trickle
But I refrained and cried a little.

You see
I'm losing it all
I'm incomplete
Broken to the core
Trying my utmost
To turn it all around.

My prayers go unheard
They're focused on her
More so that God
Will I be struck down?

The answer to your question
Is yes
I'm unwilling
And fear ridden.

Make me a drink
Grab me a lover
Sentence me to life
In their arms.

I'm not the cause of all my problems
She left me boiling in the summer sun
Dry in the mouth
Dry on the mind.

I'll commit to the life
I've been given
Just give me another drink
From the fountain of my poison.

I Am Such A Common Cold

Hell has overtaken me
Burned me, these demons scratching,
I'm cut, bleeding out,
Crimson fingers and eyes.

There's pain riffling through me
Broken pieces of hope
Scattered like gum wrappers
On the city pavements.

I'm focused on nothing
Hopelessness carries me off into the darkest of rooms
Summer is long off
Winter bites, the cold snap,
Buries deep.

Can I imagine a great life?
Full of snapshots of greatness
Flowers that bloom radiantly
No.

But I try to escape even when skating on black ice
Outside the bubble of truth
I'm ready to cave in and accept my fate.

Are you there?
Beautiful one
Or has the bitterness killed the buzz
And the vibe.

I am such a common cold
Rattling through bodies I hate
I'm such broken man
With broken knuckles.

What's keeping me alive?
Is it the thought of success?
The last dash attempt at creating magic?

Pathological Mess

Was I born to fight?
Run towards the light
Practise magic when it doesn't exist
Torment myself with lack of sleep
Dance drunk and feel the wrath of smacking skulls.

The world is a pathological mess
Deep in modern compulsions and vindictive natures
I stand and look on at the rat race
Where people contest over the last piece of hope.

I struggle to form bundles in my head
Where all my dreams should be
Nightmares are instilled and shock me into waking
up
Drenched in sweat.

I'm confined to my own woes
Stuck to the leather seat
Mania strikes twice
My mind is a castle for them all to reside
Those pincer wielding thugs
They shoot cannonballs and talk loudly
Spreading their callousness.

My brain is a pathological mess.

You

You're a stranger
An enigma
Natures challenge
Standing at the edge of oblivion.

The drunk in the picture
Is me
Those days I spent languishing
Suffering, ailing,
Dreaming of chipping away at the addiction
That was consuming me.

But you
You're a mysterious one
A superstar
Scrawling on bathroom walls
Wearing blood red shoes
Rattling against the status quo
Fresh out of suburbia.

I am a source of maliciousness
They say
A disaster
A brutalised monster
With broken wounds
Oozing poison.

I am not what they say
I am a man on the warpath
For reasons close to my heart
I can reassure you and this godforsaken world
I'm a noble, disenchanted traveller,
Saluting the birds which fly through the smog
In this industrial wasteland.

You,
Yes you
You're a character
Frightened of silence
And stricken by the past

We could come together
And waste away
Or we could chisel through to
A utopia.

Starless Sky

Heartbroken and dissolving like a pill upon a wet
tongue
My horizon is dimly lit, I can barely see the face of
the traveller,
Who I think may aid me in my pursuit of
revitalisation,
She could be my magic, or she could be a curse
darker,
Than a starless sky.

I imagined I'd be in a good place by now
Where people would love me for me
But I'm still searching for a spark of trust
And warm hands to heat my cold spirit.

The streets are heartless, but I'll still wait,
For that person stuck in the distance
She's carrying a rucksack,
It might be full of gemstones
Brighter than the sun.

But,
Hesitation forces me to confide in my own bitter
dreams
I want to disband and feature in this dangerous but
compelling world
Where I can edge through and stand amidst the roar
Where I can feel a refreshing breeze.

She comes closer, I feel comfortable,
Fables coursing through my mind
Hope building blocks, emptiness filled with
confidence.

Bright Lights and Ghosts

There's a heart in you
Buckling under the pressures of life
There's a heart in me weak and breaking under the
weight of stressful situations.
We crafted dreams so majestic that we thought we
made it,
Like two lovers escaping burdens, but we're stuck
in chaos,
Forever stretching forward for solace.
The hillside is burning like our love, and the wine
has notes,
But it's cheap and our stomachs are hurting,
But we're drunk enough to stand the pain, drugged
enough to see bright lights and ghosts.
You say to me that disbanding will keep me alive,
As I'm stuck to you like a plaster blotted in blood,
And you say that we should call a psychiatrist to fix
my head,
A mind blackened by the venom of demons.
The last of wine has been drunk,
Our brains are smoked out,
And it feels like the world is crushing my body
I'm seeing things too, like faces, in the distance,
Frightening visages smiling jubilantly,
And my heart can't take no more.

Thankfully they disappear from my vision,
Fading into the sky, and you're craving to say
goodbye,
As you place your head onto my shoulder,
Your warming body heats my soul, but I know
we're breaking.
The city will not be the same without you, it will
discolour, and it will be grey.

Meet Me Halfway

I heard that you were unstable, catching common colds,
And breathing heavily and coughing like a hardened smoker
Although you scorned me, I want to guide you from the heat of hell,
Disperse your pills down the sink hole and bury your past.

You can shunt me if you want, but you're a brother,
Nestled between life and death, proving that you're not coping
Under the weight of powerful vultures in a mind so muddled
And twisted.

I'll follow you into the dark, with a churned up stomach,
I'll search for the light in your squalor of a one bedroom apartment
In a city where junk is more accessible than prescription medication.

You're hurt and I know this, you feel like a crutch that is useless,
A commander of nothingness, a degenerate pulling the last straw
It can all change, not in an instant, but we can purposefully kill the aftertaste
And the workings of your cravings.

Meet me halfway, and I'll commend your heart.

Itchy Bedsheets

Pain exists in both of us
Carried in our guts and minds
We're swallowing pills, feeling jaded,
And stuck in a whirlwind of hopelessness
Forever placing our hearts on the line.

Throughout these dark days, we're sweating life,
And lying on itchy bedsheets, speaking to gods,
In our heads, and the devil on our shoulders,
They're debating, but we're doomed, already lost in
a loop of
Mundanity.

By injecting junk in our arms, by smoking our
brains,
Pickling the livers that used to withstand such
waves of pills and liquor,
We're slowly moving closer to the end.

You slip into a dream or a nightmare
Your eyes twitch, you create noises,
Frightening screams of terror,
And I lie beside you gripped into submission
In a spell, I can't thwart them seizing my brain.

Them?
Those kings of the mind
Those creatures of the damned
Their hearts pulsate I can hear the disgusting beats
Prolonged sounds of danger.

Fountain Of Empathy

I heard a sound of clashing demons
In my own head, they're breathing heavily,
Clawing at my honest thoughts, startling the angel,
That once sat there drinking from a fountain of
empathy.

The fountain is dry, so dry,
Like hands filled with sand,
The demons eat my soul and my chance,
Of recovery, I'm an empty shell,
Drinking moonshine from a plastic bottle,
Scorning the world through eyes that used to see
bright lights.

And the streets are eventful, full of life,
I'm standing by the shop window,
Looking at expensive bottles of whiskey,
Wishing it would travel through my pores.

I'm killing time, time which could be spent,
Kissing love into my estranged lust,
A borderline beast of ferocity, but a saviour,
Who brandished a weapon of security at the enemy,
The greed, and the perpetrators, who stole my light.

She was also a teacher to me, a livewire,
Dusting our house with sweet smelling dreams,
But, I can't see her through this crowd of drunks,
They're posing a threat to me finding her,
Although, she'll probably be sniffing powder,
And drinking her second liver.

I'll probably just reach out to oblivion.

The Stars Are Cheap

There's a heart attack brewing
I feel mystified and desperate
My insides oiled up in alcohol
Today is a not a great day.

Morbid thoughts mount the curb of my mind
I'm usually fast a pulling myself out of disarray
Now I can't escape the pain and where it takes me
So I crack open another beer
Destined to hit the oncoming traffic
That is fear.

I'm never calm
I'm always playing with fire
And life
Crying over her and the darkness which
Creeps up on me.

Tonight the question needs answered
Am I going to die young?
Subside and not propel
Cascade into the depths of hell.
Or will I turn away
From the liquor store
Draped in bargain basement prices
I wish to contain the cravings
And the notions
And these interfering emotions.

The stars are cheap
More so now
As I'm too drunk to admire their significance
I'm a mess
With a face harsh, and not smooth enough to caress
With those pretty hands
Jennifer you're too good for me.

In A World Gone Mad

The world is a strange place
Coffee is more important than love
Rage is more common than subtle dreams
And we're counting coins to make ends meet
When there's millionaires making money from war
and peace.

The last of good ones
Are nearing extinction
There's far too much hopelessness
In a world gone mad.

The social media trance
Has caught us all
We're clicking buttons
To start a virtual assault.

The children of today
Don't know the battles of yesteryear
They're suited to modern ways
Looking for gold, shrugging their shoulders,
At swollen luck.

It's time for us to abstain
And stand up and construct our reign
Hold up our hands
And make the world great again.

I see the world through drunken eyes
From dizzying heights
Up here on the roof
Staring at the motorway
Popping pills for an instant thrill.

Sick Harmonies

Penetrating through my cranium,
Your words, your sick harmonies
They aren't gratifying but deeply hazardous,
For my mind to take,
You quickly depart from the room which didn't hold
you
You fasten your seatbelt in a lavish car and go faster
than
The speed of light, lifting your spirits by leaving me,
Crawling on the marbled floor
And I can't envisage a more vindictive outcome.

Misty Dreams

You are a behemoth
Towering over my sins
You are a sign of destruction
A cannonball pulsating in volatility
Breaking through hospital walls where my head
rested.

You stood over me
When catastrophe took my words
When the blood curdled on my favorite book
When the fruit rotted next to me
Apples turning brown and then black
They festered quickly.

My mental state is judged
Ghostly figures appear from shadows occupied
By you
They're toothless, speaking in a foreign dialect
Dancing to sad songs that flood the hospital radio.

Everyone is waiting for my cranium to crack
To reveal dark anecdotes and misty dreams
They're intrigued by my disease
A condition only crazy artists would know.

The sheets itch, the drip drips,
The tears fall
Caught up in the sick bowl
Residue from weak senseless eyes.

I wish to be shown the door
To be let free and assured my life will bloom
You stand again
Ticking every box
Deeming me unfit for a world on edge

You're the doctor of pain.

Badly Drawn Dreams

Share with me
A moment of slenderness
One which may pass quickly
Timing is crucial
Peace is vital to halting grey hairs
Upon young heads
Love is a fundamental potion
In this chronicle which takes place in
A room we have sat in for days.

I light a cigarette and wash down a pill
For the ages
With a certain brand of whiskey
Swaying to the sound of voices
Outside these unpainted walls
The hollers keep us weak at the knees
Shout, scream, shout, and repeat.

We're dredging through our own minds
At times we're stuck in a cycle of badly drawn
Dreams
The colors have been drowned out
Black spots cover the white
Of these blinking eyes.

Aliens do exist
In this apartment block
They're speaking for the colony
Spawning and shifting
And we're levitating.
Up here
We feel alive
Down there
Our bodies stand
With fingers pointing at the void.

Up here
We'll stay
Until the pill
For the ages

Wears off.

For That I'm Apologetic

My heartbeat belts in my chest
I'm not cold or overly warm
I'm in between these feelings
I'm more than tired
Trying to seclude the fragmented pictures
Of ghosts and old flames in my head.

The bedroom is a space where I can rest easy
The world outside is far more of a rush of anxiety
Painstakingly attacking the harmless ones
And the people who choose to harm
It doesn't pick its faction, a minority,
It spreads across the world and into the core
The bodies, the minds, the heart.

I haven't been out in days
I'm spending too much time clashing
With loved ones and the wall
My knuckles bleeding into water
That storms through the kitchen tap
I wasn't a mishap, I meant to release my wrath,
And for that I'm apologetic.

Depression is a monster savagely breaking the
resolve
In my head it tinkers and imprints voices
And noises, it battles and is triumphant
It's ingrained in me and I can't splatter it like an
insect meeting its
End.

The light turns into night
And I'm crossing off boxes
Another day I have survived the onslaught
Of a million dark faces and legs which spring into
life
And yet I see spots of truth trying to form a frame
It might be a sign that I'm not always going to be
afraid
Of my own destructive ways.

It Can Be My Time

If my heart could bicker it would tell me a story of
broken trust
If I could stamp on anxiety like hard boots on
concrete
If I could crush it, eradicate it from my mind, my life,
Then I'd be a complete person.

My dreams faded at the age of eighteen
I was drunk and out of mind
My legs could barely carry me
I was caught in drama, walking towards oblivion,
Trying to silence the voices and to dim the blinding
lights.

At night I feel the tensions of the day
My heart belts, my mind plays tricks on me,
I feel the sharp demons pummel my head
But I compete with them
Showering them in words and thoughts.

The world is a chaotic place
When you're travelling through it
Its core is profoundly exposed
To me and the dreamers and darers.

My optimism is clouded
Clarity is covered
I claw through the over-skin to reveal
My world.

I edge closer every-day to energy
But I'm tired of cluttered intentions
I want to bury the feeling of being trapped
I want the world to know my name.

I'll escape the room
That holds me in
I'll travel to distant places
Where music binds us
Where it connects to my weird brain.

I'll scatter these empty bottles of beer
I'll dislodge any urges
I'll be a master of words
I'll support the starving writer.

I need to follow the road
To redemption
Overthrow these obstacles.

This can be my time
If I let it.

Blurry Eyes

Blurry eyes can see enough of you
Drinking bleach from a bottle cap
Enough to burn your insides,
Why do you want to fade away?
Hanging on the coattails of an angel,
She's let you go, it's not your time.

Yesterday you were dancing to the vinyl player
Saluting the sounds of the past, jubilant and praising
the world,
For its resilience, the rain hitting the window pane,
Dripping down the glass, cleaning off the debris.

You stopped the music, and you started to listen to
the wind,
Shifting and spraying rain across the street,
Blowing down street cones and bins, causing havoc,
But we were safe in this shell, our little cocoon of
warmth.

After you drank the last of the wine, you nipped my
arm,
Demanding more, became angry and disorientated,
Pushing me to the edge, crafting stories in your head,
Manipulating me, staring straight into my dazed
eyes.

I couldn't give in, I couldn't let you win,
This life isn't a joke or a charade,
But you burst my lip, the blood, the bitter taste,
Running inside my mouth.

And then you corrupted your insides,
With bleach.

Mind Bending

Your music is accessible, your heart is purring for
more blood,
The melody is riveting, and this room is bathed in
empty bottles,
And sheets of paper written in red ink, lyrics of
heartbreak,
Appear to jump off the page in this drugged fantasy,
We find ourselves immersed in.

Youth has been diminished into dust, we're growing
old,
Wrinkling faces scare me, and my own frightens
me,
When I look in the mirror, I wonder where the years
have gone,
Frames of photographs lie on the uncarpeted floor,
Broken and the glass is sharper than serrated knives.

You play a song which fills me with euphoria,
We're both under the influence, the big thumb
pressing down on us,
Our livers pickled, and should be on show to put off
the drunk generation,
Warning signs begin to show, cracks begin to
surface,
But you play technical notes and scream out mind
bending lyrics.

I dance around you and the mountain of debt letters,
My eyes shut, my dreams aching to be put on show,
But I keep them to myself, I don't want to grab the limelight,
Or soar up the pecking order with velocity, I need you too much.

The ambulance takes them away, the man and woman on the street,
Overdosed, and willing to die in each-other's arms, but they'll be revived,
And placed back on the spot, desiring more narcotics, peeling their skin and screaming for paradise to gather them up in its warm giant hand.

Empty bottles stare us down, we crave more to pound our insides,
Love won't shield us no more, and the little book of spells is false,
There's no magic here, there's no remedies, but the music is the foundation, which holds us afloat, triggering kisses and warm embraces,

It takes my breath away…

Dreams Dislodged

You hung onto me
As we walked through blustery winds
Our eyes waterlogged and our dreams dislodged
No rays of sunshine or bread to break with honest
people.

The thunder claps in our hearts begin to seize us
We're not well, nor are we able to withstand more
pain,
I've taken you too far, you should run back to safety
Into the arms of those who made you, the people
who swore to,
Carry you through life unharmed.

You wanted to come with me
To see the world
We're in over our heads
Aimlessly walking, penniless,
Tapping the shoulders of the rich
But they spit rage and ridicule.

A motel room is all we need
Comfort and a place to confide in
We can't buy integrity, we can't win over every
person,
Who walks by us, we're somewhat invisible but
crave to be invincible.

The walking wounded offer us a sleeping bag
We refrain from taking their only form of defense
We've came to the conclusion that we're homeless
With not enough strength or depth in our hearts,
To change it all.

Embers

It's rightfully yours
The radiance of the sun
But you can't have my heart
Yet you stand on my chance
To reconstruct my life, from the ashes,
From the embers that show in a wood fire's dying
hour.

Hazards chased us from the start
Bringing us down to a level
Where rats roam and eat scraps
In a gutter so dark and joyless.

And we met in a dim lit room
Brought together by alcohol and a needed push
For love and the sound of clicked fingers,
So infectious, deeply reassuring.

Glorifying a fumble in the night, kept us sexual,
But my dignity was shattering, my hopes and drive,
My innocence disregarded, and my stomach
churned,
I became lost in my own tears.

Beneath me you are not, we are equal,
Bemused by how this bond broke so swiftly,
Like a motorbike revving through the air,
And leaving tire tracks, and people shook,
By the total velocity.

We looted each other of dreams,
You began to drink, you began to scream,
Out words of venom, and I would succumb to your,
Animosity, so I would drink too, hating the way it
tasted,
Hating how I felt in the cusp of morning, but I knew
I had to,
Fall like you, to feel downtrodden, and to gain
grazes from scraping my knees,
Across the pavements outside our private hell.

You returned to me at 6am, shaken, your perfect
jacket crumpled,
Your lips broken, your breath stank of vodka, and
never before did I feel so,
Guilty, as you looked into my eyes, bewildered by
my reaction to your crisis.

I wrapped you up and told you to fight for us.

Limping Through Suburbia

Floating into this addiction
Trying to fight
My way through this box of tricks
Trying to confirm a day to feel normal.

If I can withstand the power of their grip
Its grip
Then there's a chance I could survive
Bottled water over my face
To wake me up, to give me a head start.

In the morning I feel the effects of death
I'm still breathing, but there's a light and there's a
burning feeling inside my chest.

The gaze from the ghost in my sight
Sends shivers up my spine
The party was a bad idea
And taking those pills was a habit
I didn't I want to return to.

Shapes of you come into the light
I can sense you
Glancing at my flaws and faults
Recurring nightmares go beyond frights,
I'm stuck in this home we built
I'm rigid, I can't move freely.

Rising up takes guts and I haven't got the energy to
ascend
Showing blood takes cuts
And my skin is showing potential.

Yesterday I limped through Suburbia
Catching common colds,
Taking snapshots of the bridge
With an old camera I bought at a store which is now
closed.

Those times I crave deeply
The outside world I find compelling

But today I stay inside four walls
Thinking of a future wrapped in uncertainty.

Perfect Little Freckle

My Powerless Hands Now Have Feeling.
Perfect little freckle on your face
Optimism bubbling in your mind
A once churned up stomach
Has calmed, the tide has stopped.

Heavenly smile keeps me enlightened
And my powerless hands now have feeling
I can lift you up from the cold ground
If you fall into a puddle, or if you feel like digging a
hole to keep yourself from the world.

I am your guide, you're my guiding light, who
cleans my cuts,
And whispers greatness into my ears
I am at one with peace.

The incoming pain will subside
When we swerve past the worst of it
Your hard etched resolve, will break the agony.

We are warriors in a world which is divided
We are titans on a planet which is dying
We are tough and thick skinned.

The barricade will hold, and our home will stand,
the dreams won't depart, and the sincerity will
prevail over heartlessness.

You're my lynchpin, a saviour of the moment, a class above those who crave war and destruction.

You're the subtle sea, and I'm somewhat like a distorted sound, but when we come together, we fight, we scratch, and we will bite.

I'm honoured to call you my friend, a monumental person, saluting goodness.

The Walls Drip With Wine

On a threadbare mattress
You count every crack on the ceiling
Your stomach churning to the sound of your belting
heart,
Inside this apartment of dusty memories and rats.

This used to be your kingdom
A temple of beauty
But now it is somewhat hollow
With not TV set, or phone to call your God.

You inspect the couch
To try and find one more painkiller
To eradicate the headache
That has been pounding for days.

The walls drip with wine
And glass covers the carpet
You cut yourself on it
Blood trickling down your finger.

You are desperate to cut away from this place you
can't call home.

Witnessing Love Bloom Like Fantasy

Walking lonely, drinking slowly,
Looking into the horizon,
The sky is red, the memories in my head,
Nipping at my brain.

They say the grass is greener on the other-side?
Where lushness overthrows the blackness
Where dreamers parade, where peace thrives,
And you know what?
Maybe they're right?

I'm stuck behind barricades
Made by my own stubbornness
I look on,
Witnessing love bloom like fantasy.

I'm cut up
Bleeding not only blood but personality
I have nothing to show for my optimistic past
I'm a pessimist clutching at old fashioned ways
Like an old man, reading the newspaper and
shrieking at
An overblown economy.

This world is overbearing at times
And I stand not proud but shrouded by hazards
I created with my own mouth and flapping hands
I'm not fit to sit and design wonders.

I'm still walking lonely, drinking slowly,
Drunk to a hazy night, my heart belting inside my
brutalised,
Body.

Despair

Angels dressed in their Sunday best
As a man is lifted in from his despair
Finally
He's laid to rest
His wish was to drink one more straight whiskey
Before they uttered the word
'Death'

He slumped on his favourite armchair
With an empty glass in his hand
It smashed
Like his dream.

He forgot how to communicate
His mouth seemed frozen shut
His family strewn like rubble
But all they did was care
And showed it with clarity.

He was fearless when he was younger
A fighter on the frontier.

Punk

Red alerts and signal fires
Bricks thrown and the establishment
Disenchanted voices echo in the coliseum of disdain
This world bleeds punk.

Utopias don't welcome the marginalized
Broken landscapes do
Forming bonds with gods of the world
Is not their scene
They would rather revolt
They would rather scream.

Music is in the bloodline
It's the life stream
For artists carrying hurt in their hearts
They scrawl on bathroom stalls
Their memories of rejection.

Authority figures drown out the noise
They're sapping the love
The purity of obscurity
The alternative emblem
An ethos built from blood, sweat, and tears.

Paper Aeroplane

Deliver me this
A note of where you are
A letter of redemption
A paper aeroplane
Please let me know
So I can rest easy.

The alarm wakes me
Still you're missing
In a morning of bleakness
The rain drips and hits the glass pane
In this ludicrously expensive hotel room.

I despise waking up without the knowledge of your
Whereabouts, I gave you a watch to tell time,
But time is passing by so quickly and I'm lost in
this
Sorrow ridden mind, thoughts of blood and guts,
Covering the road to California, a car crash, a bus
crash,
A collision, or even a killing, I'm stuck in
desperation.

The colourful life I lead, is darker than meat,
Past its best, the lavish lifestyle doesn't cut it
anymore,
The pivotal piece of the puzzle is gone, you're
gone,
As the wind picks up, as the rain blasts the
pavements,
The weather hits red, the sirens in my head,
Pulsate and gather pace.

I need verification, a piece of truth,
A light shone on my grey face,
Not a half-hearted news report.

I need my other half
Before my fragile heart dies.

Process Eludes Us

We expected more from this significant change in
direction
We knew we were crossing over to the other side of
our love
Bracing ourselves for a storm which carries painful
memories
We're not looking for honesty to catapult us into
peaceful realms
We're looking for closure, a chance to reflect on
these inconsistent years,
Years blotted in tears.

We proved we can fight and overcome hurdles,
But a spark of progress breaks us
Process eludes us, and we're on the ropes,
Hanging on tightly to keepsakes and photographs,
Of younger days, of drunken escapades, kisses in
autumn.

New York looks swollen with snow today
The cold snap burrows deep and we're unequipped,
For this walk of redemption, a stroll to the inner
sanctum of relationship,
Advice, where professionals try to stick us back
together, and put us back out into,
Society.

It's a bleak time for us, like frost killing the warmth,
Like bed bugs biting at our skin when we sleep,
And the rust on the spanner in the workhouse

Isn't as brittle as our struggle.

We meet darker days, prolonged days where
nothing great happens,
We meet sunny days,
Where the baked pavements are warmer than our
love
We meet couples immersed in their crusade to
spread their lust
But we refrain from partaking in such sugar-coated
dramatics.

Heavenly days haven't returned, and we haven't
fixed us,
We feel fatigued and drawn in like a gaunt face
All walls of truth are collapsing around us.

Box

Shredded cardboard boxes
And salty tears
Those boxes contained photographs
Of important years
When family values were intact.

She's lost now
Ripping up paper notes
Swirling in the air
Outside her apartment block
At 4am
Trying to reconcile
Drinking coffee to keep herself awake
The vultures are still asleep.

The light is waiting come alive
The darkness closing off
The night crawlers retreat back
Into the gutters
And she's thinking
About her life
And how it has panned out
Does she deserve to feel alive?

The train roars overhead
The smell of freshly made bread
Is a sign that morning has come.

She's frozen but prefers it
She hates the warm climate
She praises the cascading rain
The thunder storms, the lightning bolts.

She often thinks about the box
The mementos she lost
The trauma she felt
The problems which were dealt.

And here comes the light
The rush of traffic
The people wearing fabric
Too expensive to have it.

On her phone is a contact
She wishes to open up to
To reconcile with
To talk about art
And why the world is
Running into oblivion like a shopping cart.

All she can think about is the box
In the dusty attic
The charms, the magic,

The only picture she had of her mother.

A Natural Embrace

I paint sunsets on walls
To cover the blood of old
And tiny hand prints.

Forward a day
And the sunset outside
Rises up and the radiance is beautiful
A natural embrace.

For me,
The darkness has not faded
It is there, embedded in my head,
Covering the dreams that had light.

And he left,
Disgraced and demoralized by his actions,
He spoke in his nightmares
Screaming too,
About the past and demons.

My heart had been shook
By alarming instances
When the shades were pulled shut
And the blood rushed to my head.

I was down on my luck
Penniless and scorned by society
Outnumbered by tainted people.

Those days are still instilled in me
Snapshots of misery.

Dear Mercy

In a state of disrepair
Clutching onto old clothes
You left to be burned
To be dispossessed from memory.

Alcoholic taste in my swollen mouth
My tongue quivers at the next drop
It burns, and burns until my eyes water
Until my fists clench and my liver screams for dear
mercy.

The approach to this pain
Is to drink more
To collide with enemies when they're not even
there
They're in my thoughts
Melting into my brain.

Stricken by ghosts on the TV set
Fear comes to me down my arm like the signs of a
heart attack
They're flying around the overflowing ashtray
Nipping at my resolve, carrying banners,
That say ''you're dead to me too''

And these old clothes may need to be burned
So I can return to a state of normality
So this room can breathe again
With your spirit dead then I can try to open doors
To an outside world brimming in chaos and beauty.

Where Happiness Floats Above The Rot

Insecure and staring into a darkened void
I give my emptiness a name
I used to pride myself on my strength
An inner strength which has been sucked dry.

I look into the eyes of a stray dog
Through them I see its pain and my own
I cry it cries
It can barely walk or bark
I can barely walk and talk.

The streets are teeming
With abandoned people
Their trust compromised by their pasts
Their eyes bloodshot and tired
Their inner strength sucked dry.

My name is angel
I feel hell bubbling in the pit of my stomach
Coursing through my bloodstream
There is fire in my belly not because of confidence
or optimism
It burns and burns painfully.

The people here are tenacious
They're gripping onto paper-thin salvation
On their bloody knees praying for a white light
One which will transport them back into a normal
life.

Standing here
Colder than most
Crying to the sound of a thousand crying dogs
I am one of these people
Marching to the beat of struggling hearts
Gnashing my teeth at animosity and confrontation
From the people who wear gold.

In time
I may see better days
I may be able to guide these dogs and people
To a place where happiness floats above the rot
Where their bellies can be full
And their dreams can be fulfilled.

To Save Their Innocence

Did you see the world today?
Full of catastrophic incidents
People fighting with their hearts rattling
To the memories that are instilled in them
But they're swiftly dissipating as stones are thrown.

The streets are on red alert
Children with dirty faces
Blinded by the light of incoming forces
They're too young to witness such despair
And they're hungry and carrying dolls with one eye
Wishing they would come alive
To save their innocence.

Standing observing brutality
Sounds of bones cracking and bodies crashing
Cars burning and paper notes flying
Love letters singed and the world laughing
For the sake of surviving.

Yearning for a bed to sleep away the pain
Craving to be welcomed and stripped of disdain
These people don't wish to have luxuries
They want soap and food
And tender love and a place to create art
To paint sunsets on walls.

And forgotten eulogies are remembered
At night they read from books written to enforce
peace
The crackle of the fire a calming backbeat
The old and young say prayers

Acknowledgements

To be a commanding poet, you must take inspiration from other poets. I have looked up to other writers I have spoken to on social media. There are so many great poets on twitter and when I saw that influential publisher Close To The Bone were looking for poetry with grit, I had to write some hard-hitting, dark, stanzas for their poetry chapbook series. I did so, and when I look at these poems, I am proud of them and a little surprised at my own abilities.

I want to thank Close To The Bone for giving these unorthodox poems the light of day. They champion great writing that is edgy and bloody, supreme in its darkness. And they not only publish superb writing, but they wholeheartedly aid their writers in getting noticed.

To be a part of the Close To The Bone family means the world. To share my poetry means the world. As an anxious writer I often dislodge myself from the spotlight and I often throw my writing under my own scrutinising eyes, but now I can believe I've got a little glint of talent.

Printed in Great Britain
by Amazon